124 Prayers for Caregivers

124 Prayers for Caregivers

Joan Guntzelman

Saint Mary's Press
Christian Brothers Publications
Winona, Minnesota

For my mother,
Eleonora Pharo Guntzelman

The scriptural quotations throughout this book are freely
adapted. These adaptations are not to be interpreted or
used as official translations of the Scriptures.

The publishing team included Carl Koch, development
editor; Rebecca Fairbank, copy editor; Barbara Bartelson,
production editor and typesetter; inside illustrations by
Vicki Schuck; cover design by Tom Lowes; pre-press,
printing, and binding by the graphics division of Saint
Mary's Press.

The acknowledgments continue on page 142.

 Genuine recycled paper with 10% post-consumer
waste. Printed with soy-based ink.

Printed in the United States of America

Printing: 9 8 7 6 5 4 3 2 1

Year: 2003 02 01 00 99 98 97 96 95

ISBN 0-88489-340-5

Contents

   The prayers in part 1 are for the times
   when you feel privileged and blessed,
   when you need direction, or when
   you become aware of the gifts and
   opportunities for growth that caregiving offers.

   The prayers in part 2 are for the times
   when you feel exhausted by the burdens of caregiving; when anger, guilt,
   sadness, depression, and even despair
   threaten to overwhelm you; or when
   you feel put-upon, inadequate, and
   sorry for yourself.

Introduction

Caregivers wear a million faces. Some are professionals who choose caregiving as a way of life. Some are ordinary mothers and fathers whose days are filled with caring for each other and for their children. Here are some examples of people in caregiving situations:

In the tumult of feelings, Jill continues to struggle with disbelief. She had no warning that her baby would be born with cerebral palsy. Three years later it still does not seem possible. Sometimes the intensity of love for her precious little boy is overwhelming. At other times, weariness and anger at her situation make Jill feel like she cannot face him, cannot bathe or lift or feed the unwieldy little body that gets heavier every day.

☙

No matter which choice he makes, Frank will be unhappy. Forty-two years together with Mary have followed "until death do us part." Now Frank feels "parted" even though Mary is still alive. Alzheimer's disease has so invaded her mind that now only her appearance is familiar. Every day he looks for a single flicker of recognition. It never comes. Frank feels frustrated and even angry with Mary when she doesn't respond to his love and care. Frank's kids suggest a nursing home for Mary to make life easier for him, but Frank knows he could not stand that either. Frank feels caught in a hopeless trap.

＊

Every Thursday Dick volunteers as a hospice lay minister. He loves the work. He meets many families suffering through the approaching death of a loved one. He shares their pain and their hopes. Sometimes Dick feels blessed when people reward him with their confidences and concerns. At times, though, Dick feels exhausted and overwhelmed by the human suffering. That's when he wonders if he is in the right place.

＊

Life is good for Barbara. She feels blessed to have a loving husband. She loves the children. But sometimes Barbara thinks that she will scream if she sees another runny nose to be wiped or diaper to be changed or basket of clothes to be washed or meal to be cooked or house to be cleaned. Caring for her family never ends. Barbara cannot understand how she can love her life and family so much that she wouldn't change them for anything, and yet still get so tired and frustrated.

Perspective

Because modern medicine enables people to survive birthing difficulties, debilitating conditions, and severe illnesses, more of us are being called upon to serve as caregivers at some point in our life. Often caregiving falls into our lap. Sometimes we readily accept it and go with it. Other times we respond reluctantly and look for all kinds of reasons that we should not be the one to give the care, but then wind up doing it anyway. Sometimes caregiving is thrust upon us in the midst of grief, distress, and rebellion. Some of us are caregivers simply to earn a living. Others of us select caregiving as a ministry.

Though caregiving brings blessings and rewards, it is seldom easy. It usually involves demanding, unpleasant, and exhausting work. Besides the hard physical work, caregivers are dealing with often complex, always mysterious, and sometimes perplexing human beings.

Caregiving stirs a mix of feelings that may be warm and rewarding one day, painful and distressing the next. In providing care, we may struggle more with our feelings than with the physical work involved. The tender moments may warm our heart, but we may be unprepared for the anger, repugnance, guilt, weariness, and despair that can also arise. Shame or guilt may step in when we experience feelings that we think we should not have. In short, caregiving has a light side and a dark side.

Rather than judge ourselves harshly, we need to remember that all kinds of feelings are natural. Accepting them and listening to them might lead us to a new understanding of ourselves. We might befriend our feelings as expressions of our humanity and of the greatness and demanding nature of our task. In serving others, we may discover that both caregiving itself and our feelings about it are wise teachers that help us to become more fully human.

Praying and Caregiving

Prayer is often described as an awareness of God's presence, and our response to that awareness. God dwells with us and among us, everywhere, at all times, and God is always present in our caregiving. After all, caregiving offers us the opportunity to carry out the biblical commandments to love God and to love our neighbor as we love ourselves.

Prayer may be a powerful source of strength and consolation. While praying, we remind ourselves that God stands with us in our caregiving. We recall that God is never absent in the rewarding times, when everything goes well and we feel full of light and blessing, nor in the dark times, when things are especially difficult. Prayer expresses our wonder and gratitude during the hopeful times, and our need for understanding, support, patience, and guidance in the trying times. Saint Paul told the Romans: "With hope, rejoice; while suffering, be patient; pray perseveringly" (12:12).

Because prayer is an intimate expression of our unique relationship with God, each of us will pray differently. God lives within us; we give expression to God's life in us through our unique love. We need to trust God's presence and pray in whatever way we find helpful.

Our caregiving can be a prayer in itself, if we approach it with attention and love. We may pray by reminding ourselves of God's presence in the large and small acts we perform every day: handing someone a glass of water, performing treatments that require complex skills, changing diapers, or simply listening. Our prayer may involve reflecting on the events of the day, marveling at our participation in the mystery of other people's lives, or grappling with our feelings of helplessness, anger, or inadequacy. We can ask God for whatever we need, or give thanks for whatever is.

One challenge in our prayer is to make ourselves conscious of the opportunities that are ours. Both the act of caregiving and the emotions and questions that arise from it can be rich sources of prayer; indeed, they can direct our prayer. Perhaps this book can lead us to an understanding of the complexity of the human interaction involved in caregiving. It is hoped that the prayers will also provide support as we struggle to find God in our caregiving.

Using the Prayers

Each of the prayers in this book is composed of a short quotation (meant to provide food for thought), a brief reflection, and a prayer.

You may say a prayer quickly, or you may find yourself drawn to linger over each section. If you have the time and the inclination, meditate on each prayer.

You might begin by praying the short quotation once. Ponder it. Pray it again several times, slowly and thoughtfully. Let its meaning touch you.

The reflections provide material for further consideration and prayer. Sometimes the questions might invite you to write in your journal or just sit quietly and ask yourself, What is this reflection saying to me right now in my situation as a caregiver?

Finally, God assures us that our prayers are heard and answered. Offer the final prayer, recalling that God is listening to you and caring for you. If you find a particular line inspiring, plant it in your memory and pray it during the day when you have moments of silence. Or pray it as you give care, remembering that each person is sacred.

When Paul advised the early Christians to "pray without ceasing" (1 Thessalonians 5:17), he knew that bringing God's Spirit into every act can make it act of love. He also realized that only God's grace is sufficient help during difficult times. The prayers in this book can assist you by giving expression to your longings, fears, hopes, and distress. They may serve as a springboard for the expressions of your own heart. As someone giving care, cherish the knowledge that the loving God is with you, kindling your spirit, warming your heart, and guiding your hands.

During Light Times
in Caregiving

What a splendid way to move through the world, to bring our blessings to all that we touch.

(Jack Kornfield, *A Path with Heart,* p. 332)

As caregivers we have many opportunities to touch others and to make each touch a blessing. When we leave only blessings in our wake as we care for those in need, we build a better world. Do we have a heart that knows the blessings we can bring to this world?

☞

O God, may the path I take in life be marked by beauty and by blessings to other people. Let me always recognize how fortunate I am to participate in the growth of goodness in this world. I rejoice in caregiving and celebrate the opportunity to help make all things whole.

God, uncover your holy face to us.
(Numbers 6:25)

What does the face of God look like to care-givers? In what sort of situations or in what kinds of people might we find it? How do we know when we have seen God's face, when it has been "uncovered" for us? Or is it always uncovered? If so, the hope in this blessing is that we will have eyes to know it when we see it.

❧

I think that you have uncovered your face to me more times than I will ever dream, my God. But maybe you did not look as I expect-ed you to look. I'm afraid that many times you were so eager for me to see you that you prac-tically jumped in front of me saying, "See me? See me now?" and I went right on because I wasn't looking. Please let me wake up so that I see you in the people I meet, especially in those I care for, and in all of creation.

"Cure the sick. Remind them, 'The Reign of God dwells among you.'"

(Luke 10:9)

We might tolerate sickness for a short period, but it distracts us from what we consider important in the "kingdom" of this world. Yet, when we are sick or wounded, or when we are close to those who are vulnerable, we tend to drop the delusion that we are in charge, that we are in control. This is when other realities can break into our awareness.

⁀

Sickness or need is a loud reminder, O God who is always close, that a different truth operates under your Reign. It's easy to be distracted from you and get caught up in the values of this world. Among the experiences that bring me back to you, the center and holy ground of my being, are sickness and disability. May I make my home with you, O God.

When we listen deeply, the great song moves through each of our lives.
(Kornfield, *A Path with Heart*, p. 322)

Greek writer Nikos Kazantzakis spoke of coming from God and of going to God and of singing to keep from losing our way (*Saint Francis*, p. 89). Perhaps the times we lose our way in caregiving are when we forget the deep song that speaks of our unity, our love, and our interdependence with one another. But the song of life flows all the time; the Spirit is always moving within us and among us. Do we listen for it, or do we allow the noise around us to block it out?

~

The music of the universe plays in my soul. Let me be aware of it, Spirit of God. May I slow down and attend to the flow of your grace-filled song. Help me find the silence and peace necessary to hear the music and share it with those who need my care. Let me hear it playing in my caregiving.

"I was sick, and you cared for me."
(Matthew 25:36)

One of the most moving and consoling scriptural verses for caregivers has to be, "I was sick, and you cared for me." This passage describes one of the standards for salvation on judgment day. Caring for people in need is a saving act. At times in the midst of our caregiving, most of us feel this and know it in our heart. Our privilege is great. This passage can console us and encourage us if we plant it in our memory.

❧

When Jesus says, "*I* was sick," dear God, you remind me of the sacredness of my caregiving. You live in the ones who are sick, and you are in me, one who cares for them. I am part of a powerful reality, the gift of your healing grace. I don't know what to say except thank you.

*In my eyes, you are precious and honored.
I love you.*

(Isaiah 43:4)

What would we do if no one was willing to
care for us when we needed help and could
not manage on our own? Those who are willing to be present to others in need perform a
most necessary service. When we are consci-
entious and loving caregivers, we are not only
precious to God but also to those for whom
we care, whether they recognize it or not.

᠅

It is wonderful, O God who is love, to realize
and accept that I am precious to you! Help me
always be willing to offer myself in such a
way that you take delight in me. May all the
care I give be an expression of your love
being shown in my unique way.

I hope that . . . the practice of wakeful-
ness, compassion, and intimacy . . . will
bring blessings to your life, that you will
have silence as a blessing, understanding as
a blessing, forgiveness as a blessing, and that
you, too, will bring your heart and your
hands to bless all around you.

(Kornfield, *A Path with Heart*, pp. 338–339)

How might our life find blessing through our
caregiving? When our heart and our hands,
our compassion and our skills, bless those we
care for, we may find wonderful gifts coming
back to us. We exchange intimacy and mutual
support with one another. We reap the benefits of an awareness that grace is in action.

☙

O loving and generous One, I am here in the
midst of your precious gifts, growing more
aware that they are everywhere. Clearly your
blessings flow in both directions—from me to
those I care for and from them to me. Wake
me up to the wonder of your presence in this
sharing of blessings: the wisdom and the
courage, the humility and the hope. May I
bless my sisters and brothers with my heart
and hands.

I heard the voice of God saying, "Whom shall I send? Who will go for us?" Then I answered, "Here I am! Send me."

(Isaiah 6:8)

Not everyone is willing or able to reach out with care to other people. Not everyone can manage the hard work or the necessary learning and skills. Some people simply say no. When we caregivers look past the difficulties of the job and the weariness it sometimes brings, we recognize our deep desire to be of service, to help others. We begin to acknowledge that we stand on holy ground. We know that what we do is more than a job.

❧

O caring God in whose hands I rest, I am grateful for the privilege that I have in my caregiving. I am glad that you "send me" and give me opportunities to care for others. Even when I feel overwhelmed, I know that I am doing what I do for you. May I always be aware that you have sent me to those for whom I care.

No matter how well trained [caregivers are,]
the encounter with another human being
who seeks relief from suffering invariably
challenges [caregivers] in ways that their
clinical training has not prepared them for.
  (John Welwood, *Awakening the Heart*, p. ix)

Something powerful happens when we
involve ourselves in the care of a person in
need. The whole encounter challenges us on
many levels beyond just the physical aspects
of caregiving. The encounter pushes us to
look at who we are, what we believe, why we
are caregiving, and how the encounter is
affecting us. Our doing mixes with our own
being and becoming.

☙

Gracious God, help me understand clearly the
challenges that come through my caregiving.
Let me greet them with open arms, and help
me welcome the gifts and opportunities for
growth that they bring to me.

Jacob woke up. Looking around, he declared, "Surely God is here in this place, and I did not realize it!"

(Genesis 28:16)

Can I wake up to this same truth? In the midst of the mundane work that fills my days in caring for another person—the smells, the needs, the discomforts, and the joys—this message must get through: "God is here in this place!" God resides in the friend, the child, the patient, the homeless person. And God works through me in everything good that I do.

꩜

God, wake me up. Keep reminding me today of your presence. If I lose that awareness when things get tough, please remind me again. May I be consoled by the knowledge that even when I forget your presence, you are still the reason that I am doing what I do.

To receive the love of God is to recognize it is all around us, above us and beneath us; speaking to us through every person, every flower, every trial and situation. Stop knocking on the door: You're already inside!
(Richard Rohr, *Radical Grace*, p. 384)

Caregivers have wonderful opportunities. Not only can we be taken out of and beyond ourselves in service to others, but we are working at the very heart of life and its challenges. Every person we care for and every aspect of our care begs us to find and return love. We do not have to go looking for the God of love. We're there!

☙

Loving God, thank you for giving me work that is your work. Thank you for putting me where I can do what you want done in this world: love and service. How exciting it is to know that you live truly in whomever you have asked me to serve: my patient, my children, my students, my clients, and in me! Praise be to you.

Wake up! Wake up! Repent! Put on a new mind. Take on a new way of looking at things! For "the kingdom is here!"
(Anthony de Mello, *Awareness,* p. 27)

We can get into trouble as caregivers when we see only what is before us and think that we are seeing everything there is to see. The same can be said about all our experiences of life. We have eyes to see, though we often perceive superficially. We may overlook the questions: What more could we be comprehending or appreciating? What is going on all around us that remains hidden unless we know how to look and listen? Our interaction with our patients or others we serve can be filled with wonder when we begin to look freshly, to ask ourselves what we're missing, and to consider the drama of each person's journey and our part in it.

☙

How many times, dear God, did Jesus say, "You have eyes, but don't see"? Help me wake up. Sharpen my perception. Show me today how to look in new ways at myself and at the persons I care for. Let me see that what I'm doing and how I'm being has infinite value. Help me find your presence in ways that I have never noticed before. Wake me up to your Kingdom, which is already here!

Each of us is given a manifestation of God's Spirit so that we may contribute to the common good.

(1 Corinthians 12:7)

Through each of us and in everything we do, through our own uniqueness, we make the Spirit known in ways possible to no one else. When we care for someone, we unite our efforts with the Holy Spirit, source of healing, inspiration, and consolation. Absorbing this fact can set our soul afire and strengthen our resolve to give care with love.

Holy Spirit, use me to manifest your love, your healing, and your wisdom. You made me unique, a special sign of your care. May I appreciate the greatness of your gift. Let me never keep you waiting for my cooperation. Let me never refuse my collaboration. Today, keep me aware of our partnership.

The present moment brings me on a plate a hot, burning, absolutely new and original message which can enrich me infinitely.
(Henri Boulad, *All Is Grace*, p. 19)

When we can find the treasure in "right now"—in every meal we prepare, every bit of help we give, every easing of pain, every act of our caregiving—we are in touch with the reality that is the ground of our being. We come to see the blessings and marvels that surround us, waiting for our awareness. Now is the time. This moment is the blessing.

❧

Timeless God, you fill up time with yourself. Help me find you in every moment of my day. Remind me that you have an "absolutely new and original message" in each moment, a message that carries infinite rewards. When I wander, keep bringing me back to the present. Open me to the message of this moment.

Through Jesus the Christ, God will fulfill all our needs—fully, lavishly as only God can.
(Philippians 4:19)

Blessings are everywhere—in our life, in our caregiving, and all around us—but we have to be looking to find them. Sometimes we set limits and decide that good things can come only in certain ways. Because we think we know how God will act, we miss all the surprises, all the ways that God's great love is available to us.

☞

Loving God, I know that it is your love in me, through me, and all around me that sustains me in my caregiving and in every other moment of my life. Let me live today as if on a treasure hunt, knowing your lavish gifts are only barely hidden, waiting for me to find them.

Here is
a test to find
whether your mission on earth
  is finished:
    If you're alive, it isn't.
                    (Richard Bach, *Illusions,* p. 159)

Caregivers are people with a mission. A mission is usually something we have to do. Missions are healthy have-to's, deep inspirations that come from God's heartfelt promptings. Even if our caregiving is something we fell into rather than chose outright, why didn't we back away from it? Maybe we sense that something important is going on here. That "something" might just be the Holy Spirit's invitation to love.

᠗

God of love, I realize that my caregiving is not only for my patients, my family, or my clients. When I really ponder what I am about, I know that my own becoming is happening through all that I do. If I feel some sense of mission in my caring, let me live it out and do it well, as long as needs be. Send your Spirit to strengthen me on my journey.

People travel to wonder at the height of mountains, at the huge waves of the sea, at the long courses of rivers, at the vast compass of the ocean, at the circular motion of the stars; and they pass by themselves without wondering.

(Saint Augustine)

What is it about us that makes it hard for us to accept and value ourselves? Has our religion taught us that valuing ourselves is too prideful or otherwise politically incorrect? It is fine for us to marvel at how well others are holding up or managing an illness or a difficult situation, but sometimes we might also acknowledge that we are wonderful!

☞

I *am* wonderfully made, O Creator, and I thank you for all your gifts to me. I thank you for what I am, what I have done and been, and all that I can do. My abilities to feel and grow and learn fill me with blessings every day, and through them increase my knowledge of you. I am deeply and eternally grateful.

It is in the intimacy of each moment that all of spiritual life is fulfilled.
> (Kornfield, *A Path with Heart*, p. 338)

To ignore or devalue the present means that we are not really living. In each moment we choose whether to be vulnerable to what the moment offers us. To be intimate with the moment—to be so attentive to it that we allow the possibility of being changed by it—is to live fully. This moment is the right time for love; this moment is the only place for joy; this moment is the only life we really have. This moment is holy.

❧

God present, may I embrace this moment and attend to it as I would my most precious friend. When I wall myself off from the present, I also block the warm connection with life and all its gifts. O God who is closer to me than I am to myself, be there when I risk opening up and reaching out. Let me know the world of your Spirit that is moving right now through my being, through creation, and through other people.

"Love your neighbor as you love yourself."
(Matthew 22:39)

Perhaps too often we forget to love ourselves as much as God loves us. We tend to be negative and hypercritical with ourselves, and we don't take very good care of our body or our spirit. We expect ourselves just to make do. If the first course in caregiving was a lesson on loving one's self, how many of us would pass?

❧

God, help me convince myself that I am worth loving. Show me how to balance genuine self-love with what I give to others. If I learn to love myself well, I know that I will also have abundant love for those I serve. Today let me think about the ways I love myself. Show me if I am trying to love others without the basis of real self-love.

We should become increasingly attentive to the details of the things and the beings around us, even to those things which seem insignificant, since nothing is without significance.

(Boulad, *All Is Grace*, p. 31)

When dramatic things happen, we tend to sit up and take notice. In fact, sometimes we have no choice—they bowl us over. What we often miss are the gifts in the little things, the details of the care we give, the persons we care for, and our own self. Maybe some big gifts are coming in small packages, but we don't open them because we don't see them.

❧

O God of great things and of tiny things, who is as present in the details of everyday life as in magnificent events, let the little wonders capture my attention. Let me look for you and find you there. Enable me to see you in the faintest smile of thanks and to find you hidden when no thanks are offered. Let me feel you leaning on me when I provide support, and hear you calling when I'm tired and don't feel like responding. Let me wake up to your presence in the details and realize that not a single thing is without significance.

A joyful heart is excellent medicine.
(Proverbs 17:22)

Joyful hearts are wonderful medicine for those who need care as well as for those who give care. When we care for those whose hearts are joyful, our burden is eased, and we can find delight in what we offer. When we come with a glad heart, our gifts are multiplied, life falls into perspective, and we lighten the environment around the one in need. We diminish the burden that weighs us down.

☙

O God of joy and gladness, shine through me and all my caregiving. Fill my heart with your joy so that I am a source of happiness and healing for those in need of my care and even for myself. Create a glad heart in me so that I can be excellent medicine.

To honor, to bless, to welcome with the heart is never done in grand or monumental ways but in this moment, in the most immediate and intimate way.

(Kornfield, *A Path with Heart,* p. 332)

No matter what the response of those we touch, every caring act brings blessings. Each day people need what we have to offer. Each situation, no matter how simple or mundane, offers us a chance to honor, bless, and welcome. With an open heart, keen listening, and some courage, we can seize the moment and care. These invitations and opportunities are hidden in ordinary places. A willing caregiver can find them.

⌒

God of mystery and surprise, open my heart to seeing and loving and bringing blessings in situations that I would ordinarily pass right over. I usually think of you and what I am about in the big times; help me find what is really here in the small, ordinary places and hidden times.

Meister Eckhart says, "It is not by your actions that you will be saved" (or awakened; call it by any word you want), "but by your being."

(De Mello, *Awareness,* p. 87)

We know that in giving care many of the things we do are very important: bringing food, giving medicines, ensuring safety, or simply being with someone. However, the spirit with which we do these things is sometimes even more important. Our spirit and our attitude in caregiving say a lot about who we are, about our "being." When we act grudgingly, we diminish ourselves as persons. When we act with a loving heart, the Spirit of God supports us.

☞

Dear God, love is the most significant ingredient in everything I do. My willingness to love in all my actions affects my being even as it reaches out to those for whom I care. Help me grow in my awareness that although the things I do are necessary, I bring the biggest gifts in my being, in who I am and in my willingness to love.

"Treat others as you would like them to treat you."

(Luke 6:31)

This simple rule of life is a basic norm for caregivers, and yet letting our feelings, worries, and preoccupations get in the way is easy. We need to rejoice when we remember that most of us want the same things from one another: respect, understanding, and someone to simply be with us when we are in need. Humility means that we accept our weaknesses and strengths, our shadows and lights. The wonderful lesson of humility is empathy, the willingness to stand in the shoes of another.

❧

O caring God who pours out love and understanding, help me spread your love around. Even when I have no power to make things better, send me courage to love, care, and respect. May I embrace humility, the honest acceptance of who I am. May I humbly recognize that I, too, am vulnerable and needy at times. Send your grace so that I may transform humility into empathy.

No one has ever seen God. However, as long as we love one another, God lives in us, and God's love comes to perfection in us.

(1 John 4:12)

Many of us who choose to be caregivers feel drawn to a job or profession that allows us to reach out to people in need and attempt to alleviate their sufferings. Caregiving can be an expression of divine love, a love that transforms our caring and brings healing in ways beyond the physical. God's love can flow through us and come to completion in the care we give.

❦

O God, you named yourself love. Help me to know a love for myself that is like your love for me. Let my love for myself be strong and honest and filled with tenderness and compassion. I want to love myself as the unique and precious gift you have created. As I love myself with full-hearted love, I will shower an abundance of love on my sisters and brothers.

Comfort my people. Comfort them, says your God.

(Isaiah 40:1)

We all have our favorite images of comfort: sinking into a welcoming chair after a hard day's work or being hugged when we are upset or frightened. As caregivers, we probably have a whole repertoire of comforting methods. But comfort has to come from inside, from our heart. Comfort begins with a gentle, warm presence that transcends our skill or gesture.

৯

Comforting God, let me be a comfort-giving person who soothes in distress or sorrow, eases misery or grief, and brings consolation and hope. Even when I have no power to change situations, help me find ways to bring comfort.

"Give, and gifts will be given to you in full measure, packed down and pressed together, indeed, running over into your lap; because in the amount you share, in that amount you will receive back."

(Luke 6:38)

An expansive heart does not bother to measure out its giving, but Christ's promise of being showered with gifts of such variety and amount that we cannot even hold them all should gladden our heart. Those who give generously will be like children at Christmas who have a long list and find that what they receive is not only what they wanted but even more!

☞

God of superabundant gifts, you return many times more than I can even dream of. I am blessed to share in a give-and-take where I can never match in my giving the blessings that return. All glory and thanks to you.

Birth is not one act; it is a process. The aim of life is to be fully born, though its tragedy is that most of us die before we are thus born. To live is to be born every minute. Death occurs when birth stops.

(Erich Fromm, "The Nature of Well-Being," in Welwood, *Awakening the Heart,* p. 61)

In all that we are and in everything that we do, we are in the process of giving birth to ourselves. Every moment of caregiving provides us with opportunities not only to support the being of another but also to contribute to our own life. Not only what we do but how we do it becomes part of our self-creation.

~

Remind me when I go to bed at night, O God who supports me in my constant becoming, that I am not the same person who got up that morning. Each day my choices have either expanded my living or shut out life. With the people I care for and in every situation, I want my attitudes, my actions, and my whole way of being to be healthy and holy ingredients of the me to which I am constantly giving birth.

The therapeutic encounter, like any intimate relationship, is full of mystery, surprise, and unpredictable turns.

(Welwood, *Awakening the Heart,* p. ix)

Intimate sharing with another is the natural province of caregivers. We are admitted into the personal and private realm of those within our care. If we allow ourselves to be vulnerable to the other, such a privilege opens us to possibilities of growth for which we cannot prepare. We may find ourselves touched in ways we never dreamed of. Perhaps our best response is a heartfelt thank you.

❧

O God who lives in intimacy with us, keep me open and worthy of the gifts of intimacy given to me by those I care for. May I never betray their trust, and may I never betray the growth in myself that can come from their gracious and mysterious gift of self. I am fortunate to be in such a privileged position. Thank you.

All of us have different gifts, depending on God's grace. If you have a gift of prophecy, use it as the Spirit prompts you to. If you are gifted to teach, teach. . . . You who do the works of mercy, do so cheerfully.

(Romans 12:6–8)

Being cheerful suggests being in good spirits. A caregiver who is in bad spirits might be a liability to someone needing care. Grumpy, sour caregivers work against themselves. How can acts of caring that are meant to be life-giving be beneficial when done without hope, joy, and tenderness? We givers of care might think about whether our demeanor and attitude —our spirit—are consistent with our intent or if we are giving mixed messages.

᠀

Dear God, I have no desire to be Pollyanna, that is, unrealistically cheerful and bright. However, I do not want to undermine my caregiving either. Help me figure out how to be genuinely cheerful. Brighten my spirits with your presence, so that even when things are difficult or painful for my patient, and even when I'm tired or distressed, my spirits can be truly good.

"Let me learn to listen, great God of the universe."

(1 Kings 3:9)

One of the greatest gifts one human being can give to another is attention. When we set aside all our distractions and listen honestly to another person, we give a powerful and precious gift. We are saying, "*You* are important. *You* are significant. Of all the things I could be attending to, I choose *you*." Along with all the necessary actions that are part of our caregiving, such a gift can in itself bring healing.

☙

Dear God, how easy it is to focus on what I know and can do for people and yet forget one of the most significant things I can bring to my relationships with others. Beyond all my knowledge, skills, and actions is the priceless and healing gift of my sincere attention, my really listening. Let me never be so caught up in the mechanics of caregiving that I forget its heart.

There is only one place where love can be found, where intimacy and awakening can be found, and that is in the present.
(Kornfield, *A Path with Heart,* p. 333)

We can love only in the present. We may have memories of people that we have loved in the past and hopes about people to love in the future, but the only time we can actually love is right now. Our real opportunity for intimacy, for recognizing our common humanity, is now. When we are with a person who needs our care, our time together offers both of us a unique, never-to-be-repeated occasion to love. No wonder some folks describe time as a parade of holy instants.

≈

Loving God, if I keep waiting for persons to be perfect before I reach out to them in love, I may miss out on loving anyone. None of the persons I care for is perfect. Neither am I. Don't let me miss any more opportunities for giving and receiving the love that even imperfect people can share. My caregiving offers me wonderful chances. With your help, God, I can wake up to these holy instants.

A joyful heart makes for a dazzling countenance.

(Proverbs 15:13)

We influence one another without saying a word. We can be lifted up or brought low by what we see in one another. Hours after someone greets us cheerfully, we still feel the effects of their pleasant smile. Someone's anger, negativity, or depression also influences us. After such encounters we feel unsettled, disheartened, or disturbed. If we think about the power we have to influence others just by who and how we are, we may think twice about which attitudes and approaches we "put on" each day as we prepare to care for others.

❧

O God who has made us to have a profound effect on one another, help me see how I helped or harmed in my caregiving through my attitudes and way of being today. Let my heart be cheerful, even when the work is hard; and let my face shine with love and blessing. Let my work and my way of being both come from a loving, cheerful, and grateful heart.

If I become a center of love and kindness in this moment, then in a perhaps small but hardly insignificant way, the world now has a nucleus of love and kindness it lacked the moment before.

(Jon Kabat-Zinn, *Wherever You Go, There You Are,* p. 162)

We can easily begin to feel insignificant when our caregiving is hidden from others' view. It can feel like no one knows whether we do a good or bad job, whether we do it lovingly or not. We might feel isolated, with little connection to anything or anyone else. Even so, we are all connected. Each of us is a unique manifestation of the same reality. Perhaps we have never realized how any movements in our own being, any changes in our ways of thinking and acting, all have an effect on every part of the universe. But we can be centers of love and kindness, and that love and kindness will spread.

᠊᠊᠊᠊᠊᠊᠊

You have created us all of a piece, dear God. We are all in this together. Everything I let myself think or do or feel has significance. My choices can contribute to or diminish the love, peace, or harmony of the universe. Send your grace so that I may be a center of love and kindness in every moment.

*Clothe yourself in genuine compassion, in
kindness and truth, gentleness and patience.
Accept one another, and when you argue,
forgive one another promptly. Over all these
clothes, put on love that unifies and com-
pletes.*

(Colossians 3:12–14)

White uniforms, scrub suits, or stethoscopes
around the neck are signs of nurses, doctors,
or other caregivers in a hospital setting. But
some caregivers never wear uniforms or sym-
bols of caregiving. How would we like to be
known? As we dress before approaching those
for whom we care, we might run down the list
of qualities and characteristics in ourselves that
tell our patients how fortunate they are to
have us caring for them.

Today, dear God, help me be clothed well in
all the inner clothes you love to see me wear.
Let me be beautiful and strong in compassion
and forgiveness. Let my gentleness and
patience come through when times are difficult. Let me find understanding and forgiveness when I am inclined to be judgmental and
angry. Above all, let your love flow through
me and permeate everything I do.

Listen! Pay attention. Now is the day of salvation. Now is the time.

(2 Corinthians 6:2)

We often dwell on what happened in the past or what we plan to do in the future. The time that calls for real attention is right now, with this person before us who needs our care. When we live in the past or dream of the future, we miss the life that is happening in the present. Right now is the most important time; we need to relish it, live in it, and appreciate it. This moment is the moment of encounter with the holy.

☙

Living God, help me always remember that now is the only time I ever have, a most precious time. When I recognize this, I can come to realize that every "now" is a special moment, every place is sacred ground, and whatever I am doing is holy service. You live now. Do not let me miss you.

What gives value to an action is not the action itself but the spirit in which it is done. Nothing is trivial, nothing is ordinary for someone whose life draws on the eternal.
(Boulad, *All Is Grace,* p. 46)

The glorious moments of caregiving—a spectacular cure, a heightened sense of specialness, a profound awareness—are few and far between. Ordinary tasks of living and serving fill most of each day. Nothing stands out. We often come and go with little variation in our days. Because caregiving is so ordinary, we can lose a sense of the profound significance of what we are involved in.

☙

God, it feels like so much of my caregiving is ordinary, mundane, routine. Much of the time I feel like I just plod along doing nothing that matters much. Today, help me see with your eyes. Lead me to know that you observe every simple thing I do, and that my caring is holy and has infinite value.

Honor your gifts.

(1 Timothy 4:14)

Though we may have many qualities in common, no two caregivers are alike. Each of us has special gifts that we bring, gifts offered by no one else in quite the same way. Are we aware of what is special about us? Are we aware of our uniqueness? Are we aware that we offer God a way of being present to this particular person that is not possible through anyone else?

⌒

God of enormous variety and infinite expression, it's good for me to think about how I stand out in this world. In the midst of all the fullness and beauty of the universe, my way of being is unique. Help me continue to grow and develop the gifts I bring to life. It's wonderful to know that when I say yes to you, I offer you a way of being in this world that you would not have without me. Thank you.

For we can only appreciate others if we can first of all see them clearly as they are, in all their humanness, apart from our ideas and preconceptions about them.

(Welwood, *Awakening the Heart,* p. viii)

One of the hazards of caring for others is that we come to think we know them. When we listen to their cries or share their worries or wipe their noses we may begin to believe that we are getting the whole picture. We see them through the filters of our past experiences with them and with others that we think are like them. We can wind up caring for someone we do not even know because we have never allowed ourselves to see the mystery and uniqueness of who that person really is.

☙

God of wisdom, may I be open to the uniqueness of those for whom I care. Help me appreciate the wonderful shades and infinite nuances of your being, O God, as you show yourself in each person. Guide me to see that I become a source of healing for other people when I open myself to them just as they are.

With deep compassion, Jesus reached out and touched him.

(Mark 1:41)

Sickness or suffering in other people often calls us to reach out to them. We touch in many ways. We touch in our bathing and feeding and massaging and moving. We touch in compassion and feeling for another's plight, and we touch in simple connection. Our touch is one of the most powerful ways that we say to others that we are with them. We, too, can shrivel and die without the caring touch of others.

❧

O God, help me always to touch with love and respect those who are in my care. And also, please touch me. When I'm weary or down, when I'm feeling alone or inadequate to the tasks I've taken on, let me know that you will feel compassion for me and stretch out your hand and touch me. Help me feel your touch today.

Remember that sentence from scripture about everything turning into good for those who love God? When you finally awake, you don't try to make good things happen; they just happen.

(De Mello, *Awareness,* p. 88)

Frequently we find ourselves making judgments about what's good and what's bad in our life. When things go the way we want them to, we decide that they are good; and when we are not happy with how things are, we call them bad. Is it possible that the supposedly bad things may sometimes turn out to be good for us? Is it possible that we grow and develop as persons through the difficulties that we call bad as much as through the times and experiences that do not challenge us?

☞

In my caring for others, O Loving One, let me stop and think about the things that challenge me, the things I do not like and would rather not have happen. Help me understand that my task is to find the good, to work through the hard times with you. If I remind myself that you are in the midst of everything, how can I see it as other than good?

If your life is not moving toward practical action in this real, living world, with other people, with the not-me, don't trust your spirituality.

(Rohr, *Radical Grace*, p. 321)

Caregiving provides many opportunities for being drawn out of ourselves, for pushing ourselves to focus on others and their needs. When we reach out to others and are willing to stretch ourselves and give warm and loving care, both we as caregivers and others as receivers of our care stand to gain in ways that encompass and go far beyond the physical.

꩜

O God, may my coming together with the people for whom I care be a time in which I can truly forget myself and enter into a union or community of growth. Let me see that my caregiving takes me beyond myself and offers a real, grounded, and practical path in my journey toward wholeness.

The essential thing is not what I do but the significance that I attach to what I do. Once that happens, nothing is ordinary any more, and the most trivial reality is transfigured and takes on a divine and eternal dimension.

(Boulad, *All Is Grace*, p. 46)

We tend to minimize the little acts of care-giving and focus on what is overtly big or significant. Perhaps we need to turn our mind around and realize that even the tiniest things we do, if done with a clear intention of good, are "transfigured and take on a divine and eternal dimension." Every single thing we do then shines with a brilliant radiance that lasts forever.

༄

Radiant God, the little things I do—changing diapers, giving a drink of water, washing faces, cleaning up messes—are transfigured in your sight and become as brilliant as the sun. I want to do all that I do as a gift to you and to those for whom I care. I want to be aware every day of the opportunities life is offering at my fingertips. Thank you for all the ways of love.

Be united in spirit and affection. Love one another with tender hearts and humble souls. Do not return evil for evil. Instead, give back blessings. You have been called to love and thus to be blessed.

(1 Peter 3:8–9)

Caregivers could use Peter's prescription to start the day. These are wise doctor's orders. Peter describes how we would want other people to treat us. His words can be seeds of virtue that we plant in our soul and recall during the day. As the seeds grow, we will truly be a blessing to those for whom we care, and we will be blessed in return.

～

So many times, dear God, I'm tempted to be less than tenderhearted, and my soul lacks humility. But I do not want to contribute to abuse or evil in this world; there is far too much already. When the times that I feel like being hard or harsh or hurtful arise, let me consciously replace those feelings with a decision to be a blessing. I need your help. Guide me to love.

To live a path with heart, a life committed to awakening, we, too, must care for whatever we encounter, however difficult or beautiful, and bring to it our presence, our heart, in a great intimacy.

(Kornfield, *A Path with Heart*, p. 338)

We may not always be able to choose what comes into our life, but we do choose what we do with it, how we handle it. The measure of our character seems to be how we deal with what we come up against: the experiences that we want and like, and the experiences that we do not want and find difficult. Each moment we have the choice to wake up and grow, or to refuse the offer.

☙

Everything that comes into my life offers me a new step in my own becoming. May I see those I care for, with all their light and shadow, as holding out to me what I need. O God, help me to view reality as you do and to welcome into my world each of these persons and all that they bring for me. May we join together in our mutual journeys toward you.

When you cling, life is destroyed; when you hold on to anything, you cease to live.
(De Mello, *Awareness,* p. 111)

Life constantly changes. Life is flow. In our caregiving we may try to cling to health and life, to whatever we call success, and to images of ourselves as competent and always correct and of our patients as our charges. When we cling too long or try to control, we may be hindering the process of life. We demand that conditions and people remain as we want them to. Such clinging denies the dynamism of life and is ultimately frustrating.

❧

O God of flowing life, let me be one who says yes to life's movement. Let me be full of life myself. May I never choose to cling to life, to block its ever changing process. I know that I am inclined to hold on to what pleases me. Help me see that when I cling I am robbing what I love of life itself.

No matter what you do, do it for God's glory.

(1 Corinthians 10:31)

Our life is jammed with a conglomeration of things to do. Caregiving is only one part of what fills our days, though it may carve out a huge chunk of time. Sometimes we don't know if we are coming or going. However, whatever is going on in our life is the raw material that we use to grow toward wholeness and holiness. Do we do all things for God's glory?

☙

I do not want to leave out any part of my life, dear God. I want everything I do, everything I feel, and every moment to be lived and shared with you. You are with me when I'm up and when I'm down, when I'm in the middle of a mess and when things are in order, when I'm at loose ends and when I'm calm and peaceful, and all the times and places in between. I hope you're ready for all this!

And so in order to wake up, the one thing you need the most is not energy, or strength, or youthfulness, or even great intelligence. The one thing you need most of all is the readiness to learn something new.

(De Mello, *Awareness,* p. 28)

All experiences in life can teach us something. Caregiving is chock-full of possibilities because it sits right in the midst of basic human needs and relationships. When we care for one another we expose ourselves to important lessons about life. Could our problem be that we don't learn anything new because we think we already know everything? How exciting it might be if we approach our patients, our students, our children, our elders, our situations, and ourselves with an open mind and an open heart that looks for what is there that we don't know yet.

❧

God of mystery, thank you for all the things I know. Help me move through my knowing, into the great mystery that is all around me. I'm aware that I can never grasp the depth of even the simplest aspect of creation, but that my seeking is of huge importance. May today be a day of excitement for me as I step back and look with new eyes at those I care for, at myself, and at everything around me.

"Blessed are those who make peace; they shall be recognized as children of God."
(Matthew 5:9)

Needing care can disturb and upset one's entire life. Entering into a situation fraught with dis-ease, we may be pulled into the upheaval. If our own life is already stressed, acting as a calm caregiver can be doubly challenging. When all this chaos joins together, when the care doesn't go well, we may feel that matters are escalating to a point of explosion. These are times when we need to remind ourselves of the deep peace that is available within us: God's peace rooted in the sure knowledge that the Spirit wants to strengthen us and bring all things to good. We can pause and recall God's loving presence, bringing the whole situation back to a place of calm.

☞

Peace of God, fill my mind and heart today, as I do my caring for others. I choose to be a carrier of peace in every situation and with every person I meet. When times are disturbing, may I bring healing peace to calm and soothe and bring myself and others back into balance. And may we all know that the power of God's peace is ever available and working for our good at all times.

I will restore your health. Your wounds, I will heal.

(Jeremiah 30:17)

Paradoxically, when we reach out in love to help heal the wounds of another, we may start changing, too. Old wounds suffered from our selfishness, false pride, and prejudices may begin to be cleansed and closed. Each attempt to help others heal also heals us.

～

I should have known, God of healing and wholeness, that you would have surprises and gifts for me as I try to take your gifts to others. You simply will not be outdone! In that case, bless all my wounds and bring them to wholeness. May my own healing wounds be a reminder and an impetus to love, care, and help heal my wounded sisters and brothers.

*Don't carry over experiences from the past.
. . . Learn what it means to experience
something fully, then drop it and move on
to the next moment, uninfluenced by the
previous one. You'd be traveling with such
little baggage that you could pass through
the eye of a needle. You'd know what eternal
life is, because eternal life is now, in the
timeless now.*

(De Mello, *Awareness*, p. 132)

Caregiving has its trappings, both external and
internal. We carry along not only our necessary equipment but also memories and experiences from the past. We might start seeing
each situation as simply a repeat of something
that happened before. The problem is obvi-
ous: Each new situation, each day, each person
is different. Life becomes more interesting, and
caregiving becomes more lively when we
approach each encounter with a fresh perception and an open heart. When we are free
from the baggage of the past, we create a new
relationship.

Because everything is eternally present to you,
O timeless One, help me live in each now,
each moment. Let me not encumber myself, or
the people I care for, with baggage and trappings from the past. Let me appreciate whatever is, when it is, and then release it into your
keeping.

*I like the archetype of the Wounded Healer,
which symbolizes that two people in a
healing relationship are peers, both
wounded and both with healing capacity.*
(Rachel Naomi Remen, "The Search for
Healing," in *Healers on Healing,* pp. 91–92)

We make a mistake in our caring when we
think that we are only a giver and that the
person in need is only a receiver. The
exchange really goes in both directions, with
each of us receiving and each of us giving. If
we can see that we are in this together—that
each of us is wounded in certain ways and
each has gifts of healing—we may come to
recognize the depth of the relationship that is
possible and the great opportunity that it presents.

∽

My God, you come to me through the people
and caregiving experiences of my life to heal
me as well as to heal others. When I recognize
that through my caring for another I am being
healed, I say yes to a real transformation in my
own thinking and in our relationship. You are
present in the woundedness of each of us and
in the gifts that flow back and forth.

I can also open my own book, my own gospel, the story of my life, to wonder at the mighty acts of God with me, since I have my own history with the Lord.

(Boulad, *All Is Grace*, p. 82)

When we're caring for people, our focus needs to be on them. However, sometimes we need to sit back and examine our own life as the place where God is meeting us. In the very act of giving care to another, as in every moment of our life, we are in the process of writing our own story. How does our story read? What are the highlights? What are the conflicts? What notable signs of God's presence have we seen? If we keep living as we are now, what will the ending be?

☞

God of history, you allow each of us to write our own story. Guide me as I read my story as it has unfolded to this point. Let me open my perception to all the ways and times you have acted in my life in the past. May I sense your presence today. Let every chapter in my story be one that you will delight in reading with me.

*We see people and things not as they are,
but as we are.*

(De Mello, *Awareness,* p. 88)

Everything is shaped and colored by our personal perceptions. Everyone we encounter or care for and everything that they do passes through the lenses we wear. Our lenses have been formed, fitted, and ground by all our experiences, beliefs, and attitudes. Unfortunately, we might start thinking that the way we perceive life is the way that it really is. Fortunately, one gift of the Spirit is wisdom—a clear understanding of how things really are. Also, as we are transformed by God's grace, we begin to see life as God does.

෴

All-knowing God, help me be awake enough to question my perceptions, especially when I am being hard on someone or negative about my experience. Show me that I can learn a lot when I remove my personal lenses and look with new eyes. May I grow to see as you see.

Everything that happens to you is your teacher. The secret is to learn to sit at the feet of your own life and be taught by it. . . . Everything that happens is either a blessing that is also a lesson, or a lesson that is also a blessing.

(Berends, *Coming to Life,* pp. 8, 177)

If life is for learning and all of life teaches, then every person we care for and every moment of our caregiving presents a unique opportunity for growth that comes only once. How sacred, then, are these moments! What might it take for us to sit at the feet of our own experiences and patients and moments of caregiving and be taught by them? Can we recognize the lessons and the blessings? Can we find one lesson in each day?

☞

O great Life Giver, you fill my days with blessings and opportunities, and you offer me myself in every moment and experience. I often mistakenly think that I need to look elsewhere for the way of holiness. Let me see that the people I care for are my teachers, that every experience I have is my teacher, and that my life offers lessons tailor-made for me. Don't let me miss the blessings.

"I, your God, offer you the choice of life or death. Choose life."

(Deuteronomy 30:19)

Throughout our life, and especially in our caregiving, we have serious choices to make. Every moment, every situation, every encounter offers us a chance to bring life to it. We choose to be life giving when we say yes to the grace of the moment and move on in health and holiness. We opt for death when we refuse the gift of the moment and choose bitterness, negativity, or diminishment of our life. Life giving or death dealing depends not on the situation but on the choice we make. God invites us to choose to give life.

꙳

Living God, when I am asked to make a choice, no matter how tempted I am to move in other directions, support me in choosing to give life. When I'm caring for my patients or anyone in need, let me be aware that the choices I make will affect them. Help me support them in their life choices, and let us strengthen one another. Physical death will come, but may I always help myself and others live fully until death.

Professionals give advice; pilgrims share wisdom.
    (Bill Moyers, *Healing and the Mind,* p. 319)

As professional caregivers, we have a wonderful opportunity to walk with others who are suffering, in our mutual journey toward wholeness. However, we can trip ourselves up when we let the professional part get in the way. All our education and experience was meant to make us more able to help, not less. Sometimes we need a reminder that caregiving and healing depend on our mutually shared wisdom, not solely on *our* skills and *our* competence. We journey together.

⌒

God, help me approach caregiving as a pilgrim. I am grateful to you, who gave me the abilities and the inclination for caregiving; to those who supported me and provided my formal education; and to all for whom I have cared, who teach me every day. But God, may I realize that despite all my skills and knowledge, effective caregiving and healing depend on sharing wisdom, not just dispensing advice. May I be a good companion to those to whom I give care, bringing to our common journey what I can contribute and accepting from them all that they bring.

You might try, just as an experiment, to hold yourself in awareness and acceptance for a time . . . as a mother would hold a hurt or frightened child, with a completely available and unconditional love.

(Kabat-Zinn, *Wherever You Go, There You Are*, pp. 163–164)

When we invest so much of ourselves in the care of others, we may have a great need to practice loving kindness toward ourselves. Though this may feel foreign to us, we can find it has wonderful benefits: self-acceptance, self-understanding, and self-love. Silence, meditation, journal writing, and self-acceptance are certainly important wellsprings for nurturing ourselves on our journey.

꿍

Even though I know you and others love me, caring God, sometimes I do not do a very good job with myself. I can be harshly critical and unforgiving of myself. Help me take some time each day to simply hold my own self in a loving, kindly awareness and embrace.

The basic work of health professionals in general . . . is to become full human beings and to inspire full human-beingness in other people.
(Chögyam Trungpa, "Becoming a Full Human Being," in *Awakening the Heart*, p. 126)

In the midst of all the things we need to do in our caregiving, we may forget that our biggest gift is ourself. We offer a unique manifestation of God's being and love to people. We make God's love present in ways that no one else is able to.

❦

O God who is the source of my being, help me to know that the most profound way I affect any other person is through my own being, through the way that I am. Enable me to see that all my efforts to grow and become all that I can be contribute to the care that I give. Help me to understand that the care I provide contributes to who I am. Enliven me, Creator of life.

I don't precisely know what you need to do to take care of yourself. But I know you can figure it out.

(Melody Beattie, *The Language of Letting Go,* p. 97)

Even though we know that we need the same things everybody else needs to be healthy, sometimes we act like it is not so. Then we wind up being overtired, undernourished, or highly stressed; and we may feel like we cannot go on in our caregiving. We may have a hard time accepting our own humanity and needs. However, we do have the ability to figure out how to care for ourselves and to choose to let go of any guilt when we do so.

꙳

God, don't let me wait for others to tell me what I need. Help me respect, honor, and love myself enough to care for myself as well as I care for my patients. When I do not care for myself, neither I nor my patients profit. Guide me past any guilt that I am being selfish when I take the time I need to rest, recreate, and relate with people who care for me.

During Dark Times
in Caregiving

Jesus poured water into a basin. He started washing and then drying the feet of the disciples.

(John 13:5)

Washing feet, wiping noses, and cleaning up messes are some of the less pleasant aspects of caregiving. Every caregiver knows these tasks. Jesus was not above such work. Indeed, he said, "'I did this to provide you an example. Follow my example. What I have done for you, do for others'" (John 13:14–15). No service should be viewed as too humble, too messy, too beneath us. True service is worthy and holy. Even so, we may need to ask God's grace to do some of it.

❧

God of stars, majesty, and beauty, as well as of dirty feet, runny noses, and messes, I offer you my caregiving in every circumstance. Help me to be as loving, cheerful, and giving when dealing with messes as I am when things are pleasant. Be my model in everything I do.

Pray for one another.

(James 5:16)

Maybe we caregivers know better than anyone
else that we need all the help we can get. We
find ourselves in situations that are exhausting,
demanding, worrisome, and seemingly unend-
ing. When difficulty confronts us, we might
wonder why and how we do what we do.
Prayer can be an amazing source of support
and strength. Not only do our patients, children, or students need prayers, so do we. We
can connect, through prayer, with the vast
numbers of others in the world whose lives
are spent in similar service.

❧

O God, you abide with suffering, needy people as well as with those who care for them.
May other caregivers and I be filled with
strength, cheerfulness, and wisdom so that we
can provide the compassion and love that is
such an important part of the care we offer.
We count on your love and support. May we
sense your comforting presence now, my God.

"So that you may have full life, that is why I have come to you."

(John 10:10)

What does it mean to have full life? Here we are caring for people who are broken or injured, helpless or debilitated, or simply worn out. We may often feel that way ourselves; we have our own weaknesses and brokenness. Amidst our own neediness, we require the grace of God. Full life does not mean busy-ness—a filled calendar or schedule. Full life implies a harmony with God's purpose.

☙

O God who is life itself, show me how externals can be deceptive. Allow me to see how even within brokenness and need, real life may be growing and coming to fullness. Help me do my part in bringing about growth to full life through the love I share with those in my care. I cannot love without your help.

Live the present to the full! Live out the moment! Immerse yourself in experience! That is the best guarantee for your preparation for tomorrow.

(Boulad, *All Is Grace*, pp. 26–27)

When we are tired and feeling overwhelmed, we might be tempted to do things halfheartedly. We assume that we are getting the job done and saving our energy too, but we wind up feeling dissatisfied. The solution seems to be to do whatever we do with all our heart and attention, no matter how weary we feel. If we are changing sheets, we change them lovingly. If we are listening to someone, we listen wholeheartedly. Then, when we finish, we can truly rest because we have nothing to regret.

∽

Timeless God, help me to realize that all of life happens in the present moment. I have only right now. Let me live every now with my whole heart and full attention. Send your grace so that I may give myself to the moment with love and care. If I live each moment well, I will be prepared for whatever life presents.

Is it possible for the rose to say, "I will give my fragrance to the good people who smell me, but I will withhold it from the bad"? Or is it possible for the lamp to say, "I will give my light to the good people in this room, but I will withhold it from the evil people"? Or can a tree say, "I'll give my shade to the good people who rest under me, but I will withhold it from the bad"?

(De Mello, *Awareness*, p. 61)

Not all the people we care for are likable, or at least likable all the time. Some are even downright unpleasant. Naturally, we are more inclined to serve cheerfully and readily those who are grateful and pleasant. Love challenges us to go beyond our natural inclinations and pour out its blessings to everyone.

☙

Spirit of love, help me to recognize that real love does not pick and choose. Fill me with the wonderful gift of charity that blesses the giver as well as the receiver. Help me become a loving person, not one who gives only when the recipient is worth it in my sight. May I view matters from your perspective, in which everything and everyone is valued.

"When two or three people gather in my name, I am right there in their midst."

(Matthew 18:20)

For most of us, caregiving is not our only job. We fit it in among many other responsibilities. Then we wonder why we have no time to pray. Can we figure out how to do two things at the same time? Because we believe that God is present in whatever we do, why not capitalize on what we are doing and make it a prayer? As we bathe a baby or sick person, we could pray, "Wash me clean of anything that keeps me from you, my God!" As we bring a meal, we could pray, "Nurture me, my God, so that I will be strong in my love for you."

᠅

O God who walks with me, may all my caregiving be filled with prayer—not only the words I say, but everything I do. I know that you are present when things are calm, but you are also present when things are chaotic. Keep me in touch with you and with what I'm doing at every moment, no matter what the circumstances. At some level in myself, help me to pray always.

*An integrated sense of spirituality under-
stands that if we are to bring light and
compassion into the world, we must begin
with our own lives.*

(Kornfield, *A Path with Heart,* p. 315)

As caregivers, we are taught to focus on the
ones for whom we care. But how can we be
compassionate to another person if we refuse
compassion to ourself? If we extend understanding and kindness to ourself, it cannot
help but overflow to others. Often our harshness toward others has its foundation in the
harshness and lack of respect we have for
ourself.

☙

O God of light and love, fill me with light and
teach me to be loving and tender to myself.
Let my compassion for myself grow under
your care for me until it overflows to all the
world. Enable me to radiate a deep and genuine love to all those in my care.

You can't stop the waves but you can learn to surf.

(Kabat-Zinn, *Wherever You Go, There You Are*, p. 30)

We may not be able to change some of the awful things we come up against. Aging, job loss, chronic illness, and family problems are part of life. Pressures from within and without seem to multiply. We feel overwhelmed and totally frustrated when we try to stop something over which we have no control. Maybe we are aiming at the wrong place. Though we may have no power to change outside forces, we are the only ones who can change our experience of them. We can learn to "surf," to accept things as they are and figure out how to deal with them.

～

It is time, dear God, that I stop banging my head against the wall of life, trying to change what I cannot change. Let me change what I can change but then let go and move on. Help me to accept the unchangeable as a given and figure out how to live with it in such a way that I'm not always in distress. In fact, surfing looks exciting. Teach me how to surf.

This moment is as perfect as it can be. Everything is right here, right now. And if I can't rejoice now, I can't know joy at all. Is my joy based on circumstances, or is my joy based on something within that no one can take from me or give to me?

(Rohr, *Radical Grace*, p. 94)

It requires great effort to recognize that each moment is filled with perfection, especially when matters are tough. And that's precisely the challenge we find in our caregiving. The circumstances that we encounter nearly always involve pain, suffering, or the lack of something desirable. If we find perfection only when everything is as we prefer, we will never be joyful. Our challenge is to ground ourselves in God, who is deep within us all. Then no matter what the external circumstances, we can be filled with joy that no one can take from us.

❧

God, joy is the infallible sign of your presence. If I really believe you are always with me, then, even when life is hard, I have reason to celebrate. Let your joy suffuse me this day and keep me aware of my connection with you. You dwell within me and within my sisters and brothers right now.

When life says no to us, it may not mean that we are never to receive the good we desire, only that our particular idea of good is in some way mistaken.

(Berends, *Coming to Life*, p. 48)

Sometimes our notions of what would be best for us and for those in our care don't seem to work out. Whatever we try, even with the best of intentions, seems to fail. Even God appears to be working against us, and we don't understand it. Where did we go wrong? Maybe those are the times when we can expand our ways of thinking about God, life, and ourselves, and realize that the mystery of living involves much more than we dream. Caregiving challenges us to look for good in unexpected places and in unwanted situations.

❧

God of wisdom, broaden my way of thinking. Show me how exciting it can be to believe that there may be more to a situation than I can see. Whenever I ask for anything for myself or for the people I care for, know that I trust in your goodness and infinite wisdom. Like Saint Paul said in his letter to the Romans (3:20), I can say that I don't even know what to ask for, but I can trust that your Spirit in me is asking for what is best. I say yes to that.

A gentle life style is difficult to maintain
when unresolved anger lurks within me.
Anger, driven underground, poisons my life.
(Adrian van Kaam, "Anger and the
Gentle Life," in *Awakening the Heart,* p. 96)

Because caregiving is often associated with
altruism and loving kindness, we usually feel
ashamed when anger boils up. We think that
something is wrong with us, that we are failures, that we should never be angry or upset
with our patients, children, or students. So we
try hard to hide our anger, even from ourselves.
We seek to present a pleasant facade. Ironical-
ly, rather than disappearing, the anger goes
underground and affects us and those we care
for in ways that take a toll on us and them.
Anger, like all emotions, just is. We do not
have to act on it.

☙

Creator God, you gave us emotions. It would
be nice if we had just joy and affection, but
we have sadness and anger, too. When I'm
angry, God, help me to accept my anger as
natural, even expected. Let me stop seeing
anger as my enemy. Rather than stifling it
and letting it poison me and my relationships,
allow me to use its energy in positive ways.
May anger spur me to seek solutions, to clear
the air, and to confront difficulties creatively.
When I accept anger openly and look for its
message, its purpose will be accomplished,
and I can let it go.

Jesus declared, "I will always be with you."
(Matthew 28:20)

Even while caring for someone else, it's easy
to feel alone, like no one knows or cares what
we are thinking or feeling. If we are professional caregivers—nurses, day-care providers,
counselors, and so on—other people may
presume that we do not need support. Whether we are happy or sad, weary or rested, attention is usually focused on the patient,
client, or child. Sometimes we may wish that
somebody would ask about us, acknowledge
us and our work.

᠊᠊᠊᠊᠊᠊᠊ᕽ

When I'm feeling low, kindly God, touch me
with your presence. You said you are always
with me. You know how I feel and what I'm
thinking and doing. Let me see how many
ways I can find you close at hand today. I can
start by simply talking to you so that I won't
feel so alone.

Even a happy life cannot be without a measure of darkness and the word "happiness" would lose its meaning if it were not balanced by sadness.

(C. G. Jung)

Darkness and light are like opposite sides of the same coin. We cannot say, "I'll take the heads but not the tails!" In fact, we know what light is because we distinguish it from darkness. When we refuse to acknowledge darkness, we limit our appreciation of light. When we accept our darkness and the darkness in other people, we lessen its power to blindside us. We know darkness for what it is when we see it, and we can work with the contribution it makes to our life.

❧

O God of wholeness, you appreciated light and darkness and declared them good. Strengthen me so that I do not run from my own darkness nor that of my patients. Even when the specter of darkness makes me uncomfortable and challenges me, show me how it can help me refine what I know and can offer. Allow me to recognize that darkness may hide the "pure gold" of a person or a situation. Let me not be put off by its challenge.

Life in front of us pulls us out of ourselves and we have to do it because it's there. That's how I see people being purified. That kind of spirituality I can trust.

(Rohr, *Radical Grace*, p. 321)

We may get pulled into caregiving for a family member or someone close. It may not be our choice at all, but no one else is available to do it. So we dive in and do the best we can. We keep hoping that things will change, but meanwhile we adjust our routines, cook extra meals, clean a house besides our own, run errands, and see that doctor visits are kept. Maybe we don't think of it as a spiritual exercise, but when did the Spirit ever exist outside human experience?

⮞

Can you make something of my experience, God, even when I don't like it much and wouldn't choose it if I didn't have to? I just do it because it needs to be done. I keep thinking that maybe I should do something spectacular, but instead I do what I can each day, and I do it as best I can. Let it be pleasing to you.

God, have pity on us. Obliterate our faults, and toss our many sins into the bottomless sea.

(Micah 7:19)

When we care for people in need, they tend to be at our mercy. They often have little control over their situation or their life, so they must trust us and depend on our skill and goodwill. We aren't always worthy of that trust. We don't always give our care with love and empathy. As a consequence, we have the power to bring more hurt into lives that are already painful. Though this is rarely intentional, only we can make the situation right.

☞

I come to you for forgiveness, merciful God. I know that accepting the trust of others means that I must strive to be worthy of their trust. At one time or another I have failed in that responsibility. Help me gain the strength to ask for forgiveness from those that I've harmed, as well as the determination to continue my caregiving with a loving and sincere heart.

"Be at peace. Be calm."

(Mark 4:39)

When we're honest with ourselves, we notice how much time we spend fretting and worrying, mulling over our "worry list." We worry about whether we're being appreciated for our care, whether our decisions are good ones, what might happen next, and on and on. In the end, if we think about it, usually all we have accomplished is making ourselves feel bad. Whereas pondering and questioning can help our caregiving and our living mindfully, worry undermines us and accomplishes nothing valuable.

᠅

Jesus, how many times you greeted people with, "Peace be with you!" Help me trade in my habits of worry for trust in you and inner peace. Each time I find myself fretting about something, plant in my mind the words "Be at peace! Be calm!" and I will know that you are with me. Gradually, as I repeat these words, may I become a peace-filled person, even in the midst of distress.

God embraces the brokenhearted and lifts up those whose spirits have been crushed.

(Psalm 34:18)

Sometimes as caregivers our work breaks our heart. We are close to the pain, sadness, and grief that sick and dying people struggle with. If we are intimately connected with those for whom we care, we find ourselves drawn into their distress. Our sense of helplessness and suffering with them can be great. But despite the hurt, we wouldn't have it any other way. Our presence and love with them is a blessing to us both.

☙

Loving God, others' suffering and sadness feel like my own. My heart bleeds with those who suffer. May my willingness to be with the suffering be a consolation to them as they make their way through the pain. Thank you for the great privilege of participating so intimately in the lives of those whom you send to me. Mend my heart and strengthen my hands.

Spitting into the dirt, Jesus made mud with his saliva. Then he spread the mixture on the blind man's eyes while saying, "Wash your eyes in the pool at Siloam." The man did so, and when he returned he could see.

(John 9:6–7)

Few caregivers escape the need to deal with the messiness of human beings. Parents never relish wiping noses. Nurses would prefer to run from emptying bedpans or cleaning up after incontinence. Yet repugnant jobs go with the territory. With all that modern medicine has to offer the healing process—medications, high-tech procedures, computer imaging— it still has not found a way to eliminate the earthiness of human beings. Jesus healed using basic, messy substances that we work to avoid. Perhaps our challenge is to find God in the way we attend to others in ordinary, earthy, even repugnant situations.

❧

God, in my love and desire to meet you, wake me up to the down-to-earth places where you are, too. Just as Jesus used dirt and spit to heal, let me know that even the messiness I encounter in my caregiving can offer me op-portunities to show my love. Though I may never enjoy distasteful jobs, I want to approach them with a willing and transforming heart. I count on your being there with me.

"Don't let your hearts be anxious or fearful."

(John 14:27)

Caring for other persons is often an enormous responsibility, even when they can still choose some things for themselves. We might find ourselves making decisions, giving medicines, even deciding when or if to call for help from someone else. We are not even sure of our own abilities sometimes. We may have great concern about making mistakes, and may fret and wonder if we are up to the task of caregiving.

☙

Dear God, it's easy for you to say that I shouldn't be troubled or afraid. But here I am in a situation that I don't always feel able to handle. And I do worry that I might make mistakes and be a source of harm to those for whom I am responsible. Help me to learn well the knowledge and skills of caregiving and then transform my worry and fear into peacefulness and love.

The Spirit of God helps us in our weakness. Even when we do not know how to pray properly, the Holy Spirit intercedes with all manner of pleading. The Spirit makes our needs clear and intercedes for all the people of God just as God wills.

(Romans 8:26–27)

Even when we're smart, well educated, and trained, we don't always know what's best. We struggle with people and situations, trying to do what we think is right in our caregiving and in our decision making. Ethical dilemmas present themselves, and we can see the wisdom in both sides of an issue. Making decisions can be the hardest part of giving care. After examining the best information available, tapping into our intuition, asking advice, and praying, we can trust in the Holy Spirit within us.

❧

O God, you sustain the whole universe. Help me to trust in you and your wisdom. When I have studied the facts, prayed, and listened to myself and to others but am still confused and don't know how to proceed, let me remember that your Spirit dwelling within me is already asking for what is necessary and best for all the people concerned. Let me know that I will never go wrong if I trust that presence within and say yes to whatever the Spirit asks.

No person on earth has the power to make you unhappy. There is no event on earth that has the power to disturb you or hurt you. No event, condition, situation, or person.

(De Mello, *Awareness*, p. 79)

Admitting that we give birth to much of our unhappiness is hard. Accepting this is difficult not because it isn't true, but because we don't want it to be true. It's easier when we can blame someone or something. In caregiving we are prone to blame our irritability, anger, or unhappiness on those we care for or on the situation, where many things can provoke unhappiness. We have to make a conscious effort to be happy. We can ask for God's help when times are tough.

☙

O God, source of joy, may your happiness always be bubbling within me. I know that doesn't mean that I will be smiling constantly, but deep down, even when things are difficult and distressing, I will be in touch with a solid and blessed base of joy: your presence and love for me. So instead of blaming others for my displeasure, may I choose to accept the responsibility for myself that you have given me.

You will be angry, but don't sin because of it. Don't let the sun set on your anger. . . . Speak only words that will support and affirm one another.

(Ephesians 4:26–29)

Anger frequently flares, even in unimportant matters. When we are intimately involved with those who are ailing, needy, suffering, or dying, intense emotions are naturally aroused in the one needing care and in the one giving it. Deep emotion wells up when life is difficult, and we struggle with big questions. In fact, to expect patients or clients and caregivers to interact without times of great emotion is quite unrealistic. Emotions of all kinds will be there. Our challenge is what we do with them.

∽

Help me to receive emotion as one of your gifts to me, O God. Let me accept emotions as natural. Teach me that it's not the emotions that are problematic, but what I do with them. Enable me to think through my responses when I'm feeling wronged or angry, and help me choose to respond in ways that I will feel good about tomorrow. Also, may Paul's admonition to "speak only words that will support and affirm" take root in my soul and guide all my actions.

No creature on earth can hide from God.
Everything lies uncovered.

(Hebrews 4:13)

Anger sometimes permeates everything about us. We're angry with the persons we care for, angry with others who don't help when they could, and angry with God for leading us into these situations. Then we feel guilty for being angry and are ashamed. So we grow angry at ourselves. We don't want God or anyone else to see us so upset.

⸕

Loving God, I know that much of my anger comes from feeling helpless and unable to bring about a better situation. Please look right through my anger and see my desire to care. Transform my anger into energy for doing good.

Emotions are fluid expressions of our alive-ness, and they are constantly changing, in-process. . . . The irony is that in trying to control them, we become controlled by them all the more. So we find ourselves stuck in their grip—which leads to more attempts to control them or to explosive eruptions that leave us further alienated from them.

(Welwood, *Awakening the Heart,* pp. 85–86)

Nobody wants to be the loser in any battle, and if we didn't battle, we wouldn't have to lose. But, as with our emotions, we set up many things as our enemies, and a battle ensues. If we can drop the battle lines between us and our emotions, if we can stand with them and hear what they tell us, the battle stops and no one loses.

❧

Dear God, don't let my emotions come between me and my patients, or between me and my desire to do good. Don't allow me to battle with them and make my life a power struggle. When they arise, let me feel them, accept them, and listen to what they tell me. For today, let me notice how many different emotions I feel, and enjoy the many nuances in my experience.

The more you resist something, the greater power you give to it. . . . You always empower the demons you fight.
(De Mello, *Awareness,* p. 147)

Sometimes our emotions are the demons we fight. When we're involved in caring for another person, we can expect that emotions will run high—for us and for our patients or children or elders—because emotions are always intense when we are suffering and in need. Joy, delight, and gladness are easy to take. Anger, guilt, and sadness are unwelcome, and we work hard to avoid them. Paradoxically, when we make our emotions our enemy and try to resist them, they tend to grow in strength and intensity, and threaten to overwhelm us. If we can accept and even befriend them, receiving their lessons and gifts, we often find that their power diminishes.

☙

O God who made me wonderfully, who gave me emotions as expressions of great richness and variety in myself, help me appreciate them as gifts and signs of life. Let me welcome them as expressions of what's happening within me and learn from them in healthy ways. May I use their energy to move forward.

"I, your God, will travel with you, and then I will lead you to rest."

(Exodus 33:14)

Days may follow days when fatigue and exhaustion never seem to ease. One job is accomplished and two more emerge. No respite is in sight, no sign that the need for care will be less. If we could just get enough sleep, just close our eyes for a while without interruption and find some rest, caregiving would not seem so overwhelming.

～

Companion God, show me how to find moments of rest in you while I wait to find longer stretches of respite. Refresh me throughout this day, moment by moment, as I do what needs to be done. Let me become creative at finding treasures of rest even in the midst of my work.

With God, anything is possible.

(Mark 10:27)

Times come when we don't want to give care anymore—not even for one more day. We don't want the burden of caring for someone else. We get tired and angry and don't understand why others don't help. We feel trapped because we know that if we don't give the care, it won't be done.

❧

O God who sees me and knows my struggles, I know I can find in you what I need to continue with the job you have presented to me. I know you can lift the heaviness that I feel and sometimes even bring some satisfaction and good feeling. I count on you. Send me patience, courage, and perseverance. Help me. Help me, merciful God.

Let nothing disturb you,
Nothing cause you fear;
All things pass

. . . .

Whoever has God
Needs nothing else,
God alone suffices.
(Teresa of Ávila, *Saints for All Seasons*, p. 128)

When we feel weary and at our wits' end,
when we feel we cannot go on, when everything we do seems to turn out wrong, when
not a word of thanks comes in our direction,
when we are angry with everyone else and
even more so with ourselves, we better stand
back, refocus, and remember that all things
pass. At these times, we need to remind ourselves of Teresa of Ávila's words. As we share
in God's work of ministering to people in
need, God will strengthen us if we call out for
help. Often calling for divine help is all that
we can do.

∾

Living God, comfort me in my distress. May
I have Teresa's confidence that this too will
pass. I know that your grace is all the suste-
nance I need, but may I believe it more firmly.
God, come to my assistance. Strengthen my
resolve, cleanse me of anger, soothe my
nerves, enlighten my understanding, and grant
me patience.

"Hold fast and have courage. Put away fear because no matter where you journey, I, your God, will be with you."

(Joshua 1:9)

Sometimes we find ourselves in places we don't want to be. Our caregiving may be one of those places. We wind up in unpleasant situations that sap our strength and diminish our hope. We perceive no way out. People need care, and we may be the only one who can do it. Every day may bring chores that we are not sure we can handle. Even if we can do the tasks, we may feel trapped between our desire to be elsewhere and our sense of responsibility. We don't want to abandon those who need us.

❧

God, in times like these I begin to feel angry, even with you. I don't want to be in this situation of desiring to be somewhere else but at the same time wanting to serve and do the right thing. Do you see my distress? If you want me to be strong in this conflict, then you have to be here with me. Be my strength and the steady ground that keeps me able to do what I must do. I have to know that you're here, or I just cannot keep going.

"I, your God, love you forever."

(Jeremiah 31:3)

Sometimes we don't do our best and feel ashamed. We get frustrated and upset with those in our care, and we take it out on them. We may do our work haphazardly, snap at them, talk curtly, or act brusquely. Then we wonder what we're doing and feel like a failure. Regret and guilt cast gloom over us. At times, we fall short of what we want to be.

～

O God of mercy and love, forgive me for my failures. Let me learn from them and work at being more like you in all the care that I give. Let me forgive myself as you forgive me, and help me to realize that no matter what, you love me. Allow me to begin again each day.

You will forget your sufferings,
  but recall them as a flood that has passed.
Your life, more radiant than the noonday,
  will make a dawn of darkness.

(Job 11:16–17)

Our caregiving may go well for a while, but then we get upset or angry about something. Our whole world becomes distorted by our distress. We make our situations worse when we act like our feelings are permanent. When we're in the middle of hopelessness, why not remind ourselves that down times are to be expected. If we don't hold on to them, they will pass like a flood.

☞

Spirit of God, teach me to accept and learn from all my feelings and then let them go. Help me remember your word is true and is meant for me. With your assistance, I can move beyond my present struggles. With your support, my life will be "more radiant than the noonday." Thank you for the hope you hold out for me.

Be assured, in all matters God works for good.

(Romans 8:28)

Despite our best intentions, sometimes we fall flat on our face. We usually feel pretty good about ourselves. Then we crash. We make a serious mistake, or we're unkind, or we neglect something we should have done. We feel terrible. We're good at giving care, but we don't know how to handle our mistakes very well. Lest we forget, we can apologize, and we can forgive ourselves. Then, as Paul says, we can "be assured" that God will work good out of our failure.

⌇

When I finally face myself and you, dear God, I have to admit it's a humbling experience. I don't like to make mistakes and am embarrassed about them. Remind me at times like this that I am just like every other human: I have the power and the ability to do wonderful things as well as to make terrible choices. Don't let me stay in the mistake or the bad feeling. Let me feel my kinship with other people, pick up, and move on. I want to help make all things good.

God does not view matters as humans do. Women and men see appearances, but God looks into the heart.

(1 Samuel 16:7)

We don't always do what we would like to do. We try to come to our caregiving with the best of intentions, but they don't always show through. Sometimes our best efforts fall flat or are rejected. We get mad and explode without thinking. In so many ways, we don't seem to measure up to what we want to be. Fortunately, God sees what is in our heart and takes into account our sincere desire to serve.

☙

God, your understanding penetrates through the externals and seeks out the heart. Let my heart be filled with love, and let that love permeate everything I do. I want all my caring to come out of love and be filled with love. Let that be so even when I don't consciously remember to say it. Help me to show it. Create a loving heart within me.

There's no way you can love until you forgive yourself for not being perfect, for not being the saint you thought you were going to be.

(Rohr, *Radical Grace,* p. 81)

Somehow we caregivers find it easy to get caught up in trying to be perfect, striving to do everything just so, and wanting people to like us. Paying attention to what other people need can get squeezed out when we are focused on our own need to be perfect. Love can be messy, so it doesn't feel welcome in the company of perfectionism. Love is much more at home with vulnerability. When we're vulnerable, we let down our defenses, admit our fallibility, and permit something besides perfect images of ourselves to enter.

⟿

Let me prepare and learn my job well, my God, and then forget about looking at myself. I want to embrace my imperfect humanity. Let me accept all my weaknesses, mistakes, and doubts, and know that my wounded patients and I have much in common. When I can find that common ground where our wounds come together, then we can share in a love where you feel completely at home.

"I am your God, and I will guide you in the direction you should journey."

(Isaiah 48:17)

Sometimes I just want to take off, leave, and hide from my responsibilities as a caregiver. I want nothing more to do with sick or needy people, or suffering, pain, and sadness. I want wholeness, health, rest, and delight. I want to enjoy the good things of this world and forget about everything that's difficult and painful. I don't want to work so hard.

❦

God of my pilgrimage, I count on you to lead me, especially when times get hard and I don't want to be here. Help me find the health, rest, and delight that are your gifts, gifts that can be found even in sickness and pain. When my feet are directed toward escape, let me see daylight where I am. May my soul be renewed by my inner journey with you.

In the desert places of your life, God will lead you to a cool oasis.

(Isaiah 58:11)

Desert places are usually harsh, hot, and uncompromising. They offer little protection from the unrelenting sun. Going into a desert unprotected, without water and provisions, is not only unpleasant but life-threatening. Sometimes caring for another feels like a desert place. The demands on our attention, tenderness, and patience can be as unrelenting as a desert sun. We may feel overwhelmed by the harshness. However, deserts also teem with life. Hidden away from the untrained eye are plants and creatures that have learned to live in the harshness and heat. We can find them if we know where to look.

❧

Dear God, when my caregiving makes me feel like I am trekking in the desert, when I feel so totally unprotected from what could overwhelm me, remind me that teeming life can be found if I look carefully enough. Make me as wise as the desert plants and animals, who can teach me lessons in survival. Show me the hidden places where you are and where you offer me relief.

I will never forget you.

(Isaiah 49:15)

Caregiving often seems thankless, useless, and forgettable. We wonder what everything is worth and what it all means. We wonder if there isn't another way, something that would feel more rewarding. We wonder why we work so hard. And we even wonder where God is.

❧

Dear God, even when I'm not thinking of you, you're thinking of me. Show me that I am never out of your awareness, that I can never catch you by surprise and find that you've forgotten me. Every single thing I do, all the care I give, every moment of my life is written in your heart. You are right here now, loving and remembering me.

"If you want to follow me on the way, you must reject selfish desires, lift up your cross, and follow me."

(Matthew 16:24)

Life is often difficult. Caregiving means that we add to our concerns by assuming some of the burdens of other people. Each situation we deal with has something that challenges us, something that asks more from us than we are prepared to give, some way in which we're asked to deny our own gratification. We don't have to look elsewhere for opportunities for holiness. We each have our own special cross, made from the unique burdens of our life.

☙

Loving God, help me to understand that my cross is made from my life. May all my burdens, even those of my caregiving, be sources of growth and good. When I am tempted to desert my responsibilities, to shirk my duties, to deny love, remind me of Jesus' words. Strengthen me to meet the challenges.

If we live as we breathe, take in and let go, we cannot go wrong.
> (Clarissa Pinkola Estés, *Women Who Run with the Wolves*, p. 163)

Things pile up, and we don't seem able to turn anything loose. We feel responsible for everything and don't trust others to do things well. In the end, with our clinging, everything threatens to come crashing down. In these circumstances, thinking about flow might help. Water that doesn't flow becomes stagnant. When air stops flowing through our lungs, we die. When we hold on to worries, questions, fears, and emotions, we may eventually burst. We need to teach ourselves to take in and to release.

☙

Spirit of God, never static, teach me to connect and disconnect in healthy ways. Let me connect with those for whom I care when our connecting is healing and grace-filled. And when I need to let go, show me how to do that with love and belief in the wholeness of myself and of the other person. Each time I inhale and exhale, may I remember that life needs to flow.

Moved with compassion, Jesus reached out his hand and touched him.

(Mark 1:41)

Tending to someone we love who has lost the ability to relate to us is hard on caregivers. For no apparent physical reason, the one we love gives no sign of recognizing us. Our heart can break every day as we hope and search in vain for some sign, some glint in the eye that allows us to make contact. We grieve daily in these situations for what we have already lost as well as for losses to come. We have two persons to care for in these situations—our loved one and ourself.

꙳

Dear God, caring this way for someone I love is agonizing. It would help me if she or he just recognized me a moment and knew that I was here. But I don't receive that consolation. Please forgive my frustration and distress. May all my love and tender care be received even if I have no sign. May the touch of my hands communicate the tenderness of my heart. Touch us both with your love and care.

Be kind toward one another.

(Ephesians 4:32)

It is difficult to care for people who give all the directions, who want everything done according to their plans. People who need help may feel a loss of dignity and self-esteem when they cannot be in charge. When they have to surrender independence, they may try to order others around even more. As caregivers, we struggle with that kind of desire to control. Sometimes we have to be in charge. Resolving the not-so-subtle battles tries our patience.

❧

I can reason things out well, God of wisdom, and it doesn't seem to make any difference. Perhaps I must realize that dealing with people who feel that they are losing control of their life is not a question of reason as much as a feeling of loss. Instead of arguing and trying to win, maybe my greatest contribution to the situation would be a little kindness. What would I really lose? Grant me the grace of kindness.

The things we can't do anything with (the useless) and the things we can't do anything about (the necessary) are always the things that connect us to the Real.

(Rohr, *Radical Grace*, p. 380)

The old, the downtrodden, the doddering, the disfigured, those whose minds are unable to connect with the world, and many other people that society deems useless come to us for care. It's hard work, and we may want to run in the other direction. But often these people have no place else to go. Their need reminds us in sobering ways of our own needs, insecurities, and vulnerabilities. They challenge us to question what we believe in and value.

⌒

Isn't it enough, God, that I'm willing to take care of some people in need? Caring for these folks is hard on me on the outside and on the inside, and I'm not sure I want all that difficulty. Maybe I'm put off by your hiding in places that don't attract me. Why do you make caring so hard?

How long, O God? Will you forget me
  forever?
How long will you hide your face from me?
(Psalm 13:1)

When we're giving care by ourselves to babies
or to persons who are unable to communicate
with us, or when no one seems to notice or
appreciate our work, we can experience a
profound sense of isolation. Such solitary
effort may prove especially taxing. These situations may push us to find another person
with whom we can talk about our experience.
At least then we can gain some perspective on
what we're doing. But sometimes we just feel
abandoned, even by God. When this happens,
we might remember verse 5 of Psalm 13: "I
believe in your faithful love; joy in your saving
power fills my soul."

⁓

I feel so alone, my God, and sometimes it
seems that even you abandon me. It gets harder and harder to continue my caring when I
feel that no one else even knows where I am.
When you hide your face from me, I'm going
to keep searching until I find you. I'll look for
you especially in a friend who may be willing
to share my burden with me. Failing that, I
will call on you in prayer, hoping to feel the
steadfast love that the Psalmist praises.

Give your enemies food if they are hungry. If they are thirsty, give them water. In doing so you will heap live coals on their head.
(Romans 12:20)

At various times the people we care for seem like the enemy. They can be difficult, refuse our help and suggestions, and have hateful dispositions. Paul makes an interesting suggestion. When we choose to be loving in return, when we don't respond in kind, we throw our tormentors a curve that may shock them enough so that they will reconsider their behavior. However they respond, we can choose loving, because our responses aren't determined by their way of acting.

❧

Wise God, you know that sometimes I need to be shocked out of the ugly behavior to which I have become attached. Help me with all those who are hard to care for. Give me the wisdom and the strength to continue to be loving to them. Maybe my kindness can help them out of their unhealthy ruts.

All people get angry, saints and sinners
alike. Feeling annoyed, angry, aggressive is
therefore as human as feeling sad, delighted,
loving, tired, or lonely.

(Van Kaam, "Anger and the Gentle Life," in
Awakening the Heart, p. 97)

Anger is inevitable in every person's life. By its
nature, caregiving involves being in undesir-
able life situations: helplessness, pain, sadness,
and need. As a result, our own vulnerability
and fear get touched. Because we work hard
to avoid situations that remind us of our own
helplessness, we grow upset with the person
who unknowingly reminds us. Awareness of
the source of our anger may help us to understand and manage our own reactions.

☞

Merciful and compassionate God, let me console myself with the story of Jesus' anger in
the Temple. Remind me that anger is a natural
response, built in and even potentially helpful
to me. When I'm angry, help me accept what I
feel as part of my own humanity—actually a
sign of life. Let me know that my vulnerability
and helplessness are not signs of weakness,
but cracks in my armor where I can most easily make contact with you. May my feelings of
vulnerability lead me to rely on you more.

An essential part of the therapeutic process with trauma victims is the building of a relationship that can serve as firsthand evidence that others can be good, that the client is worthy despite the traumatic experience, and that trust rather than mistrust may often be appropriate in one's approach to the world.

(Ronnie Janoff-Bulman,
Shattered Assumptions, p. 162)

Sometimes our caregiving has repercussions beyond those we usually consider. When we care for someone whose belief in life has been shattered, the way we relate may help them find their way back to a healthy life. The support of people close to the victim seems to be one of the biggest factors that contributes to healthy adjustment.

❧

When I care for persons who have lost their trust in people and in life, please, God, give me the tenderness, respect, sensitivity, and reliability that will help restore their trust. Let me stand in for you in a strong, healthy, and caring way, so that they can choose life again and know that it is good. Help me to understand the enormous significance of my trustworthy and loving presence.

"Blessed are those who grieve: they will be comforted."

(Matthew 5:5)

Perhaps we need to spend more time mourning than we realize. As caregivers we have the privilege and the pain of dealing with loss of all kinds. It's healthy and right that we attend to those losses. Comfort comes only when we have grieved. When we refuse to mourn we swallow up our grief and hold it in our heart, where it compounds until we're willing to let it flow. Our grieving can be a strong and healthy acknowledgment of how deeply we value the gift of our life.

❧

O God, you hold my life in your hands. Help me to realize that my grief is a sign of how much I have treasured my blessings. Only when I have refused to connect can I avoid grieving. I want to be able to acknowledge what I have been asked to let go of, to grieve in whatever way is healthy for me, and to move on with my life, open to what is still to come. Take my loss into your keeping. I especially want to mourn and let go of my grief for

_____.

Life is not the way it's supposed to be. It's the way it is. The way you cope with it is what makes the difference.

(Virginia Satir)

How much of our time do we spend with the "if onlys"? If only this patient was more pleasant. . . . If only my family knew how hard I work. . . . If only somebody would take care of me once in a while. . . . We can waste an enormous amount of time and energy in such wishful thinking, but it doesn't help us cope. In fact, this kind of thinking usually makes us feel worse! We *do* have real power within ourselves to look at the way things are, to make whatever changes might be helpful, and to figure out how to deal with things we cannot change.

⮪

I don't want to spend too much time moaning, dear God, though maybe a little or even a lot is all right when my struggles are hard. Most of the time I want you to help me jump in and make the most of my life. I've been blessed with talents, abilities, people who love me, and you, my God, and I know it's my job to figure things out and do the best I can. But I rely on your help.

Jesus noticed that Mary and those who came with her were weeping over the death of Lazarus. Their distress touched his spirit and moved him deeply.

(John 11:33)

Caregivers must sometimes minister in the midst of great sadness. Whether the one we care for is a relative or a dear friend, or whether we're moved by the suffering of others, we sometimes find ourselves caught up in grief. We're torn between letting our own tears flow or keeping them back so that we can do what needs to be done. Sometimes our tears can be a gift, but sometimes we need to delay our own grieving. In either case, one price of caregiving is often grief.

꩜

Caring God, Jesus loved so much that he was moved to tears by Lazarus's death. I, too, am moved profoundly by death, loss, and suffering. Just as Jesus' tears expressed his grief, let my own sharing in grief with others be a real gift to them. Help me to know when my tears minister to others and when I need to find different avenues of service. Either way, be with me in my sadness, God of all consolation.

Tears not only represent feeling but are also lenses through which we gain an alternative vision.

(Estés, *Women Who Run with the Wolves,* p. 158)

The struggles in our own life or in the sufferings of our patients or clients may move us to tears. And for whatever reason, we feel embarrassed or weak, or that we shouldn't burden others with our sadness. This holds true especially for career caregivers. Is it possible that tears are a blessing? Can we consider the benefits of letting our tears flow? Perhaps tears communicate when words fall short. Perhaps tears carry pent-up feelings and allow them to wash freely from our heart. Perhaps we see more clearly and more honestly through our tears. And perhaps our tears give comfort to the families and friends because they show that we honor their loved one.

No matter what I've been told to the contrary, God-with-us, I thank you for the gift of tears. I feel deeply sad at times, and nothing expresses what I feel in quite the same way. Nothing allows me to move on more freely than letting myself cry. Somehow I come to see things differently when I'm honest about my feelings and let them flow through my tears. May my tears also be a consolation to others torn by grief.

The challenge is to find such a secure footing in life that we can be truly loving together; so that we can, in fact, truly love, rather than use and abuse each other.
(Berends, *Coming to Life,* p. 44)

One of the dangers of caregiving is the possibility of using the person in our care for our own purposes, for our own gratification. We don't consciously set out to do this, but we might find it creeping into our expectations and actions. It is easy at the times when we aren't feeling rewarded or when we would like to blame our patient, client, or student for being ungrateful or uncooperative. We may hope for some gratification from our efforts, but we have to be careful of expectations. Expectations ungratified can lead to discontent, carelessness, and even manipulation.

Life-giving God, love doesn't depend on reward, but I like to know that I'm appreciated. I want to give my love and care freely, with no strings attached. I want to receive whatever good gifts return to me, but allow them to be unexpected gifts. Please keep me clear and aware of the times when I expect my own needs to be met by those I care for.

The only way someone can be of help to you is in challenging your ideas.

(De Mello, *Awareness*, p. 35)

We caregivers have a hard time coping with rejection of our knowledge or skills. We come with good intentions and preparedness, but the persons we care for are ungrateful, do just the opposite of what we suggest, or say that they don't like what we offer. It all feels like a low blow to us. We are tempted to turn the rejection in the opposite direction and storm off to nurse our own hurts. It's so hard to recognize the opportunity to grow that comes in the challenge.

⤸

If what I know or believe is never challenged, O God of wisdom, it will solidify and stop growing. But it's hard to see challenge as a gift. It's difficult to let go of my own position of authority and responsibility with those I care for, and I know that others are not always right. So maybe the best I can do is to look at my ideas when they are under fire, to reconsider what my beliefs and ways of doing things are. Maybe just in my open looking, new life can come.

We are like a breath,
  our day, like a passing shadow.

(Psalm 144:4)

If only our day felt like a puff of wind, if only
we had some sense of this work passing when
we labor day after day in trying circumstances.
Occasionally we have to remind ourselves that
our perception of time is relative. Time flies
when we're delighted and drags when we're
in pain or distress. Maybe we need to stand
back and think about what this present experience will seem like when it's all over. It, too,
will pass.

☙

My God, I know this trying time won't last
forever; it just seems like it will. Instead of
living for the future, let me bring life to this
moment, because it is the moment you have
given me. Sure I hope for a better time tomorrow—that's only human—but help me to
improve this moment. Wake me up to how
quickly life is moving, how many yesterdays
have already passed.

What often seems to release an emotional tangle is not catharsis per se, but letting our feelings speak to us and reveal what they are asking us to look at, what they are telling us about how we are relating to our life situations.

(Welwood, *Awakening the Heart*, p. 83)

Intense human interaction provokes a deluge of emotions. When emotions are pleasant, we delight in them. When emotions such as guilt, anger, repugnance, revulsion, shame, distaste, or dislike swamp us, we try to push them into a dark closet in our mind. However, emotions can teach us if we invite them to. They're rumbling around inside anyway, even if we are holding them behind a door of denial. Once we open the door, we might look them in the face and ask, What about me brought you around?

᠗

Living God, teach me to be open to the lessons of my emotions. Let me see that every welcome or unwelcome reaction of mine offers a gift. May I discover what each of my responses is telling me about me, and decide how I can turn that information into a step forward in my own becoming and in my own serving. Instead of expending energy by holding the door closed on my feelings, may I open it and converse with these teachers, even if I don't like them.

We must strike a balance between what we do for ourselves and what we do for others, learning to receive as well as to give. For if we only give and never receive, we get out of balance.

(Elisabeth Kübler-Ross, "The Four Pillars of Healing," in *Healers on Healing,* p. 128)

It's so easy to get out of balance. In taking care of another person we can get so caught up in what we're doing and what we ought to do that we forget our own needs. For instance, we need a respite, a time to recuperate from all that we put into our caregiving. No matter how important our task, we need to replenish the energy we spend.

☙

Re-creating God, you know that all of life is giving and receiving, letting go and taking in. Help me keep in balance. Enable me to recognize that caring for my own needs is not selfishness. You want me to grow and be whole. Let me know that my patients and I are important in your eyes, and that we both need my loving attention and care.

Few situations—no matter how greatly they appear to demand it—can be bettered by us going berserk.

(Beattie, *The Language of Letting Go,* p. 161)

When tasks, feelings, or decisions stack up, we worry that we're losing control of ourselves and of the situation. Sometimes we entertain the temptation to scuttle our responsibilities and cut loose. At other times we feel that if we give in to our emotions, they will take over and pull us down, and we will never find our way out. A strategic, temporary withdrawal can be the best strategy to avoid a headlong retreat.

๑

At certain times, wise God, I need you to wrap me in your great serenity and calm, take me by the hand, and lead me step-by-step to stable ground with you. Abandoning my duty recklessly does no good to anyone; neither does fleeing my fears and needs. Teach me to pull away for quick, quiet moments inside, where I can breathe deeply, acknowledge your presence, breathe deeply again, and re-create myself.

Cast your cares on God, who will sustain you.

We have to unload the burdens of care, even just for a while. Sometimes we feel so weighted down that we're not sure we will ever be free of the heaviness. The words of the psalm should remind us that the responsibility is not all ours. God cares for our patients, clients, children, and students, too. God not only sends us strength but can inspire us to find help from other people and to discover creative solutions to caregiving dilemmas.

☙

O God, your nurturing love encompasses me and the people I care for. Help me to trust your support. I know that you and I are joined in our caregiving, and that I can count on you to be here, sharing the burden. When the load gets too big for me to carry alone, may I not be too proud to call on you for help.

The greatest revolution in our generation is the discovery that human beings, by changing the inner attitudes of their minds, can change the outer aspects of their lives.

(William James)

Our mind gets us into trouble sometimes. What we think, how we talk to ourselves, and our attitudes all direct our perceptions of everyday life. When we view ourselves as put-upon, treated unfairly, angry, misunderstood, or unappreciated by those we care for, our reluctance to care for people grows proportionately. When we continue with these thoughts and attitudes, our care is not helpful to our patients or to ourselves. We all suffer the consequences. Fortunately, as William James suggests, if we change our attitudes, we can alter our behavior. Saint Paul says the same thing: "You can be transformed by transforming your mind" (Romans 12:2).

～

God, help me to remind myself that I can choose to approach each situation in healthy ways. Allow me to understand that no one can transform my mind but me, and that the choice isn't determined by what's going on outside of me, but by what is within me. I want to be a loving, compassionate caregiver no matter what anyone else does or says. Help me to make that so. Give me the support I need to carry out that resolve.

It is our job to identify our needs, and then determine a balanced way of getting those needs met.

(Beattie, *The Language of Letting Go,* p. 365)

Caregiving is not a question of either-or: either our patients, clients, children, or students get what they need, or we do. When we find ourselves getting out of balance, we don't abandon those we care for and take care of ourselves. Nor do we continue to give care until we collapse. The challenge for us is to make it both-and. This requires some creativity, reflection, and wise advice. Consider your needs; list them. List your responsibilities. Weigh, sort, ponder, pray, and plan. God will help.

☞

Sometimes it's tempting to work until I drop, dear God, and then see what others would do. However, I know that nothing would be gained by this approach. Let me be wise and humble enough to understand and accept my own needs, and to ask for help when I require it. Inspire me with creative solutions in my caregiving balancing act.

"You need to draw away and rest for a while, by yourself."

(Mark 6:31)

Even Jesus took time off. In our service we forget to stop and reflect on what we're doing and why. In order to stay healthy and be clear and soundly based in what we're all about, we need to draw away sometimes. We need to rest and nurture our spirit. When we take this time in genuine self-love, we can stay on track in our journey toward wholeness and become better caregivers in the process.

⤳

Holy One, present to me in my rest as well as in my caregiving, help me maintain balance in my life. Grant me the insight to understand and accept my need for rest and my need to give care. Both sides are integral parts of my journey. When I am giving care, let me do it wholly and with love, and when I am resting, let me give myself that same attentiveness and love. If I get frazzled and feel guilty, may I remember Jesus' words, "Draw away and rest for a while.'"

Having boundaries doesn't complicate life; boundaries simplify life.
  (Beattie, *The Language of Letting Go,* p. 168)

Some of our problems in caregiving arise when we lose our awareness of what we can do, what we're responsible for, and what we can control. With the best of intentions, we become enmeshed in situations and lose our ability to maintain a healthy perspective and sense of ourselves and our patients. No one profits when that happens. A periodic reflection on our boundaries provides helpful guidance when demands come from all directions.

⸙

Though you love and care for me, my God, you also give me the freedom to make decisions. Help me to see that though you permeate my life in ways that are beyond my knowledge and awareness, you want me and others to be ourselves. Help me hold on to a healthy sense of myself and my boundaries, and allow others—no matter how much in need—to do the same.

To keep a lamp burning we have to keep putting oil in it.

(Mother Teresa)

We expect ourselves to be able to keep caring for others as though we have a bottomless well of energy. The truth is that though God provides abundant energy, we need to tap into that energy through reflection and prayer. And our own body needs care through exercise, sleep, and healthy meals. We serve through mind, heart, and body. We need to find our own ways to replenish the oil in our lamp.

❧

Remind me, God of light, that when I give of myself, you are always ready to refill my stores, but I need to take time and be open to receive you. Let me recognize that you are present as fully in my times of replenishment as in my times of service. Help me meet you there.

I lift my eyes to the mountains.
  Where is help to come from?
My help comes from God,
  who made heaven and earth.

(Psalm 121:1–2)

Caregiving demands lots of physical and emotional energy. It is frequently hard, draining work. We don't have an unlimited supply of energy, and so we must figure out what the source of replenishment is for each of us. The principle of burnout is that more energy goes out than comes into a system. Do we think about the ways our energy is replenished and build them into our life? The Psalmist spoke of "lifting our eyes to the mountains" to find help. Are we built up again through time in the mountains, meditation, relaxation, outdoor activity, reading, exercise, prayer, creative expression, or a combination of many opportunities?

☙

Dear God, when I spend myself without replenishment, I wind up being no help to anyone. I know what nourishes and refreshes me. Thank you for these gifts, and may I turn to them readily. I recognize that I have far more to offer when I am vibrant and full of life than when I am burned out. Praise to you, my God.

Sometimes I go about pitying myself,
and all the time
I am being carried on great winds across the
sky.

(Ojibway, adapted by Robert Bly,
News of the Universe, p. 249)

When times are hard for us and we feel caught
in lonely places, we so easily slip into self-pity,
sadness, and wistful wishing that things could
be different. If only we didn't have to. . . . If
only people were grateful. . . . If only we
could. . . . Would it make a difference to us
if we knew that we weren't seeing the whole
picture?

❧

O God of mystery, help me to see beyond the
problems and get beyond self-pity. Your spirit
can fire my imagination and heart, inflame my
soul. Somewhere deep inside me resides an
awareness, even if only a tiny inkling, that
there is always something more. Maybe if
I just sit in that silent space with you, God,
I will find what I already know.

Acknowledgments *(continued)*

The quotes on pages 16, 19, 22, 33, 37, 47, 60, and 84 are from *A Path with Heart: A Guide Through the Perils and Promises of Spiritual Life*, by Jack Kornfield (New York: Bantam Books, 1993), pages 332, 322, 338–339, 338, 332, 333, 338, and 315, respectively. Copyright © 1993 by Jack Kornfield. All rights reserved. Used by permission of Bantam Books, a division of Bantam Doubleday Dell Publishing Group.

The material paraphrased from Nikos Kazantzakis on page 19 is from *Saint Francis* (New York: Simon and Schuster, 1962), page 89. Copyright © 1962 by Simon and Schuster. All rights reserved.

The quotes on pages 24, 43, 44, 54, 74, 88, 101, 122, and 131 are from *Awakening the Heart: East/West Approaches to Psychotherapy and the Healing Relationship*, by John Welwood (Boulder, CO: Shambhala Publications, 1983), pages ix, 61, ix, viii, 126, 96, 85–86, 97, and 83, respectively. Copyright © 1983 by John Welwood. All rights reserved. Reprinted by arrangement with Shambhala Publications, 300 Massachusetts Avenue, Boston, MA 02115.

The quotes on pages 26, 57, 86, 91, 111, and 119 are from *Radical Grace: Daily Meditations by Richard Rohr*, edited by John Bookser Feister (Cincinnati, OH: Saint Anthony Messenger Press, 1993), pages 384, 321, 94, 321, 81, and 380, respectively. Copyright © 1993 by Richard Rohr and John Bookser Feister. All rights reserved. Used with permission.

The quotes on pages 27, 38, 56, 61, 63, 66, 69, 82, 98, 102, and 129 are from *Awareness: A De Mello Spirituality Conference in His Own Words* (New York: Doubleday, 1990), pages 27, 87, 88, 111, 28, 132, 88, 61, 79, 147, and 35, respectively. Copyright © 1990 by the Center for Spiritual Exchange. All rights reserved. Used with permission.